DOMINATE

The Practical Formula To Building A Profitable Writing Career On Social Media

Stanley Umezulike

DOMINATE

The Practical Formula To Building A Profitable Writing Career On Social Media

First published in Nigeria in 2021 by **IfèAdigo**
10 Magic Pond Street, Jikwoyi, Abuja.

Copyright ©Stanley Umezulike, 2021.

All rights reserved.

No part of this publication may be reproduced, stored or transmitted in any form by any means, electronic, mechanical, photocopying or otherwise, without the prior permission of the publisher, except in the case of brief quotations embodied in reviews.

The right of Stanley Umezulike to be identified as author of this work has been asserted by them in accordance with the Copyright, Design and Patents Act, 1988

Cover Design: **IfèAdigo**
Layout: **IfèAdigo**

Foreword

The advent of the Digital Age brought certain freedoms, some of which were felt in the Publishing Industry. Traditional Publishers, who had been the gatekeepers of the publishing world for so long and had enjoyed certain domination, suddenly lost their powers. With online platforms, anyone and everyone could write and publish their book without the aid or permission of traditional publishers.

But they had one more super-power; the trust of a worldwide audience, financial power, and the means to reach a global audience, amounting to a wide scale of readers ready to buy whatever book they publish.

This is something that digital publishing did not give to writers. It is also not something that can be bought in the market. Therein, they retained their power.

However, as the digital age advanced and social media began to gain prominence by becoming a primary tool of communication, writers began to experience a never-seen-before advantage.

Primarily, readers are curious people. The after-effect of reading a good book is a desire to connect with the writer for multiple reasons, one of which includes first-hand information on new releases by the same author.

With Social media making the world a global village, new lines of communication and opportunities grew for the writer and the readers. Suddenly, a writer could interact with readers directly. With quick wit that is often necessary in this industry, writers began to use this channel to attract and retain loyal readers, to build a tribe or community of people all over the world with a common desire to read more of their books.

This was the Aha! moment.

But the Digital Age also came with certain disadvantages, one of which is a proliferation of authors all over the world. Suddenly, the publishing industry became a crowd. Millions of people became writers, and with such a crowd, how could one become seen and heard?

The need to gather a tribe of loyal readers, to build a community, to be visible in the crowd became an urgent one. Writers were no longer faced with the problem of publishing but a problem of visibility.

Social Media was the power, but how exactly does a writer wield such power effectively?

Stanley Umezulike has successfully used social media to launch his writing career. As a traditional and self-published author, Stanley has used social media to amass for himself a community of loyal readers who believe in his stories and are ready to buy his books whenever he publishes them. His service as a coach and the founder of a fast-growing writing community is also a huge strategy. How did he do it, and more importantly, how can you replicate his success?

This book provides detailed answers to these questions and more. Social Media is a powerful tool for writers, but there is still a need to learn how to use it effectively. Stanley has provided a much-needed resource for writers all over the world.

    Glory Abah,
    Author and Creative Writing Coach.

Table of Contents

Foreword 3
Acknowledgement 7
Dedication 9
Introduction 11
Chapter One 13
    From a Shy Newbie Writer to an Award-Winning Author 13
        I Struggled Because I Lacked Direction 16
        Trial and Error Method with no Results 17
        The Turning Point 18
        The First Set of Critique was Harsh 19
    Gaining Recognition and Building a Vibrant Online Writing Community on Facebook 20
        Writing Exercise 23
    Chapter Two 25
        The Writer in the Age of Social Media 25
        The Statistics Are Mouth-Watering 26
        Writers Can no Longer Ignore Social Media 27
        Social Media Enables You to Build Visibility 28
    Social Media Enables You to Easily Connect with Readers all Over the World 29

Writing Exercise 31

Chapter Three 33

Building an Effective Brand as a Writer on Social Media 33

Ten Simple Ways to Build an Effective Brand as a Writer on Social Media 36

Writing Exercise 46

Chapter Four 47

Ten Simple Strategies You Can Use to Promote and Sell Your Books on Social Media 47

Writing Exercise 52

Chapter Five 53

Bonus - A Virtual Tour of Stanley's Writing Process 53

From Idea Generation to Publishing 53

Self-editing tips 58

How to pick your editor 60

Writing Exercise 61

Conclusion 63

About the author 65

Acknowledgement

My deepest gratitude goes to the Almighty God, to Him be all the glory.

This book would not exist without the help of a great team who brought what was once an idea into reality.

My special thanks goes to my great friend, brother, and co-founder of IfèAdigo Publishing Company, Akwaeze Louis. Thank you for your invaluable input and support at every step of the process.

Major thanks to my wonderful author friends, Christiana Agboni, and Leila Kirkconnell, who took time out of their busy schedule to edit the first draft of this book. Thank you.

To my mentor, Victoria Sanford, I'm grateful for your guidance and encouragement. Thank you for helping me take a bold step in my writing career.

I'm thankful to Glory Abah, for taking time out of her busy schedule to read this book and write the foreword. God bless you.

I'm grateful to all the members of Prolific Fiction Writers Community. You are the best.

I owe a huge debt of gratitude to my family. I'm grateful for your support. I'm grateful to all those who helped to bring this book to life. Thank you so much.

Dedication

This book is dedicated to all writers who are determined to achieve their writing dreams and win in this digital age.

Introduction

In this digital age, one question is at the lips of most writers all over the world; how do I promote and sell my works on social media? To do this is simple, build the right audience on social media, convert your audience to customers, and they will keep buying the books you write. But how can a writer achieve this? By building an effective brand as a writer on social media.

Years ago, the idea that a writer could build a profitable writing career using social media was farfetched. Today, it's not just writers who are doing it; brands and organizations have used social media to build lucrative businesses and thrive.

Building a profitable writing career on social media is not overwhelming like many writers think. It's actually very simple. Today, the internet is flooded with sophisticated strategies and big words on how writers should achieve this. Many books on personal branding are written with words, jargon, and terms that most writers struggle to understand. I'm not a fan of sophisticated strategies. I prefer simple and practical strategies that work.

Before I started writing this book, I discovered that most writers struggle to build the right audience on social media who will buy their books. Here's the worst; it's difficult for most writers to get access to books that show them how to harness the power of these platforms and build a profitable writing career.

In this book, I'll hold you by the hand and show you ten simple step by step processes I've applied in my own writing journey, which helped me to move from a shy newbie writer to an award-winning author, writing coach, and founder of a vibrant global writing community on Facebook. These are simple strategies that will help you build a profitable writing career on social media to dominate the global stage.

You will also discover ten simple strategies you can use to promote and sell your books on social media to generate a massive income.

In addition, there's a bonus for you; you will get a virtual tour of my writing process and see how I generate ideas for my books. The tour will take from idea generation to publishing.

If you are a writer seeking to win and dominate in your niche in this digital age using social media, then this book is precisely written for you.

Join me on this beautiful journey. I hope that what you learn in this book will help you build an effective brand as a writer on social media, and achieve amazing success in your writing career. I also hope this book helps you gain clarity and move with confidence and purpose in your writing career.

Cheers to your success.
With love,
Stanley.

Chapter One

From a Shy Newbie Writer to an Award-Winning Author

Before I became an award-winning author and the founder of a vibrant online global writing community on Facebook, I used to be a shy kid who loved to hide in the crowd.

However, I'd always enjoyed reading and writing right from when I was young. One of my childhood's sweetest memories is of my late father (may his soul rest in peace) giving me books and newspapers to read.

At the age of five, I remember one week when he returned from one of his travels, the first thing he did was to give me a Saint Anthony Magazine.

"Chukwuebuka, read the story in the last page. You will love it," he addressed me by my Igbo name.

My eyes sparkled. I collected the magazine and turned the pages fast until I reached the short story section. I finished the sweet short story in five minutes and went to his room to ask for more magazines. From then on, my father continued to give me magazines and newspapers and buy books for me. I remember he'd open the newspaper and tell me to read the literary section. At that time, I didn't know that my father was laying a strong foundation for what would eventually become my writing career.

My father made me develop an interest in reading and literature. When I was about to enter high school, he made sure I entered a school that was known for its culture of reading and writing. At high school, I was the kid who many of my classmates laughed at and mocked because of how skinny and shy I was.

I was shy, and was afraid of being in front of the public. I preferred to keep to myself and stay in my own little world.

I had few friends. The books I read were my best friends. I knew the characters more than I knew my real friends.

Then, I would be in school for one week, and no one would know I existed. If it was my turn present at Monday Morning Assembly, I'd beg one of my classmates to help me out and stand-in for me. I was an introvert, and I couldn't help it.

Things got worse when I was in my SS1, and the school authorities finally gave their verdict about me. At the end of the third term that year, they wrote in my report card, "He hides in the crowd," and my father scolded me with fire and fury.

When I became a senior, I made more effort to come out of my shell, but deep inside me, I knew the battle wasn't over. However, as I grew during my teenage years, I wanted more out of life. Sometimes, I would feel empty.

A part of me knew I could grow up to achieve great things in my life. I had big dreams I wanted to achieve. One of them was to write the kind of books I loved to read. But to achieve my ambitions, I could not continue to hide. I needed to come out of my comfort zone.

At the age of fourteen, I wrote my first book—a ten-page novel with the title, *It's Too Late*. If I see the book today, I'd laugh at myself, but that was the point when I knew I would be a writer. For the next four years, I wrote for fun, and my fans and cheerleaders were my family members.

In high school, I would go to the school library and escape into the world of the books I read. When I became a senior in high school, I became one of the best literature students. I read all the books I could find in the library. I read novels, history books, biographies, and books about life. Then, my friends and I would go to the post office at Onitsha in Nigeria and buy used novels from the book vendor. This was in 2007 when one of my classmates introduced me to American novels.

When I started reading books written by Sidney Sheldon, John Grisham, James Patterson, Nora Roberts, Danielle Steele, Da Brown, and Clive Cussler, I couldn't stop. I'd never read books like that before. It was like I was watching a movie. Those books were more interesting than some of the books our literature teacher told us to read.

At sixteen, I searched for books like that which had African characters, but I couldn't find any on the bookshelves. One day, at the age of eighteen, I asked my classmate. "Felix, we've read so many books written by American authors. We've read many novels featuring an FBI agent chasing criminals and solving criminal cases in America. How can we get a novel like that featuring a Nigerian Police officer or a Department of State Services (DSS) agent solving cases here in Nigeria? I have not seen any on the bookshelf."

My friend, Felix Odibe, stared at me for a moment and said, "It's because we don't have such books here in Nigeria."

"What should we do?" I asked.

Felix met my gaze. "We should write it."

My eyes widened. "What?"

"Yes, those bestselling authors don't have two heads. Let's write the kind of books we love to read," Felix said.

We had this discussion when we were about to finish writing our Senior Secondary Certificate Examinations. After that conversation, I took up the challenge of writing my first novel.

I wrote it in six months and finished it at the age of nineteen. The title was *The Shock*. It was a mix of political thriller and crime fiction. It featured two Nigerian agents who were members of the National Anti-Terrorist Unit (NATU). It was the kind of book I loved to read. I loved it.

I published it five years later, in 2013, when I was a third-year student of the University of Nigeria, Nsukka.

I Struggled Because I Lacked Direction

After selling the book in schools where I lived, I didn't know how to sell it to a wider audience. Worst, it wasn't published online. It was published only in paperback. Then, I had no idea of how digital publishing worked or how to promote my work on social media. My Facebook profile then was cluttered with posts about my football club – Barcelona FC, and rants about

Nigerian politics. I had no idea of how to build an effective brand as a writer using social media.

There were two reasons why I struggled to build a profitable writing career at that time. The first reason was that I was a shy newbie writer who was afraid of being in the spotlight. I thought I could achieve success just by having the writing talent and writing more books. The second reason was that I had no mentor who would guide me and help me navigate the world of writing and publishing.

I only had friends who had the same knowledge I had about writing and selling books, which was nothing at the time. Then, we believed that the only way we could succeed as writers was to meet top VIPs who would help us get our books recommended for Secondary schools in Nigeria. And if we were lucky, the book would be recommended for JAMB, a national examination written yearly by over two million students before they could be admitted into Nigeria's tertiary institutions.

Trial and Error Method with no Results

For several years I stayed within the web of my ignorance, and I continued to do a trial-and-error method that bore no results. Then, I didn't know about the importance of social media for writers. I didn't know how the publishing industry worked. I didn't know about the opportunities that existed for writers in the digital age. At a point, I stopped taking my writing career seriously and just wanted to get a job, marry, have children, get old and die.

The Turning Point

The turning point came at the beginning of 2017, when I decided to try again, this time, by joining writing communities on Facebook after reading a post that advised writers to do so on Google. In January 2017, I joined writing communities on Facebook, and that singular decision transformed my writing career. My eyes widened when I saw writers on social media who had achieved amazing success in their writing careers. They had reached where I wanted to go. They had thousands of readers who bought their books. They approached writing with professionalism. They had built effective brands as writers on Social Media. Their books were published on a global publishing platform called Amazon—a word I heard for the first time in 2016. The question I wanted to ask them was simple: how did you do this?

I began to follow them online and study the strategies they used to get more readers and promote their works on Social Media. The entire process appeared to be overwhelming, but I kept learning. Next, I took a bold decision and started making posts in these Facebook groups for writers. I asked questions about the things I didn't know, and I was surprised when I received answers from writers who wanted to help me.

I threw my shyness and fears out the window and began to connect with writers all over the world via Facebook, Instagram, and Twitter. When I discovered there was such a thing called beta readers, I became bolder and requested to send my stories to them to read and give me feedback. They did.

The First Set of Critique was Harsh

The first set of critiques was harsh. However, it opened my eyes. All those years when I thought I was the best writer in the world with my family members as my fans, I didn't know that most of what I had written was trash. I began to unlearn the wrong things I learnt over the years and learn directly from these authors who had achieved amazing success in their writing careers. I paid for writing courses and began to invest in my writing career. I bought books on writing craft. I became intentional about my writing career and learnt about what would help me gain clarity and build a profitable writing career.

In 2018, I got a mentor, Victoria Sanford, an American author and a kind-hearted woman who believed in me and guided me every step of the way. Three months after meeting her, I got a publishing contract from Love Africa Press, a traditional publishing house based in Epsom, Surrey, United Kingdom.

I am forever grateful to Victoria Sanford. She was the angel I needed in my writing journey. She taught me how to write synopsis and query letters and how to submit my work to publishers. She also taught me how to write for an international audience.

Victoria showed me how to promote my works on social media. I learnt from her and other authors from different parts of the world how to harness the power of these platforms and use it to build a profitable writing career.

Soon, I began to build the right audience on social media and generated my first seven figures from my book sales. I used the money to pay for my school fees during my master's program at the University of Nigeria, Nsukka. Today, I have readers on social media who love my brand and are willing to buy the books I write.

Between 2018 and 2021, I landed four publishing contracts and published four books. This meant that I made more progress as a writer within those three years than I had my entire writing career.

Gaining Recognition and Building a Vibrant Online Writing Community on Facebook

In 2020, I decided to help other writers excel in their writing career, and in that year, I trained over 3000 writers, helping them gain clarity in their writing career. After benefitting from many author's wealth of experience, I decided to pay this forward and help writers get to where they deserve to be.

My goal is to continue to transform lives through storytelling. My mission is to raise a new generation of fiction writers who would understand how to write for an international audience and dominate the global stage.

I'd worked with some of these amazing writers and found out that they had great writing talents. I also discovered that many of them would have achieved more if they knew what to do if they knew the right steps to follow regarding their writing dreams. What they needed was a little guidance, and they would take the world by storm.

My aim was to bridge that gap and help aspiring writers and writers with the guidance and information that would enable them to excel in their writing careers.

This propelled me to create my own writing community on Facebook called Prolific Fiction Writers Community (PROFWIC) on the 1st of September 2020. Today, it has become one of the fastest-growing writing communities on Facebook, with over 5000 members. Since I created PROFWIC, I've been getting amazing testimonies from writers who said that PROFWIC had transformed their writing career. Others said that PROFWIC brought their dead writing careers to life. Still, others told me that PROFWIC helped them gain clarity and gave them the tools to excel in their writing careers.

In recognition of my work of transforming lives through storytelling and sharing my stories with the world, I was awarded "Top 40 International Leading Youth Award 2020," in the best author of the year Male Category, an initiative organized by Make Mee Elegant Foundation to commemorate the 2020 International Youth Day and celebrate youths across the world who have been truly outstanding and impactful in their various fields. The award and other recognition I had received over the years were a tremendous honour to me. However, I know that the reward for hard work is more work.

With such an award comes great responsibility, and I do not take that for granted.

I've long dedicated myself to the service of humanity—to adding value to the lives of others. I will continue to help writers gain clarity in their writing careers. I consider this book my best gift to writers in this digital age. I believe those who follow me on this journey will gain all they seek and build a profitable writing career that will bring them wealth, happiness, and fulfillment.

This is a brief story of my writing career. From growing as a newbie writer who avoided the spotlight and knew nothing about the writing and publishing industry, I have grown to become an author who built an effective brand on social media and who has a writing community on Facebook that helps writers gain clarity and excel in their writing career.

In the following chapters, I will show you why writers should no longer avoid social media. I will show you ten step by step processes that would help you build an effective brand as a writer on social media. I'll also show you the ten best strategies you can use to promote your book on social media.

Writing Exercise

1. What did you learn from my story, and how can you apply it in your writing career to start getting the results you seek?
2. What were the new habits that helped the author transform his writing career?
3. What decisions will you take today that will help you create such new habits for yourself and begin to excel in your writing career?

Chapter Two

The Writer in the Age of Social Media

If you are reading this, you should know this digital age is the best time to be a writer. Many years ago—before the internet, getting published was difficult. Traditional publishers were the gatekeepers of publishing. This means if your book is not accepted by a literary agent or a publisher, it will remain in the closet for years until you get a big break.

Worst, if you are unable to get one, you will not achieve your writing dream. Those traditional publishers published the works of few writers and had a wide readership base. Even if you decide to publish your book in a printing press by yourself, it would be difficult for you to reach thousands of readers who will buy your work.

However, the internet and technology changed everything. The beginning of the twenty-first century saw the emergence of digital self-publishing platforms and social media platforms. The first among the digital publishing platforms was Amazon, which made book publishing easy for writers. They made it easy for writers to publish their books and get them in front of millions of readers. When Amazon emerged, other platforms started. Today, many digital self-publishing platforms such as Okadabooks, Ingram Spark, Barnes and Noble, Bambooks, Kobo, Apple Books, and more are available for writers to publish their works online.

One of the first social media platforms to emerge and reach one billion active users within its first ten years is

Facebook. Today, there are other social media platforms such as Instagram, Twitter, Whatsapp, Youtube, Tiktok, Clubhouse, Signal, Telegram, and more, where writers can meet and connect directly with readers and get them to buy their works.

But there's an important question we need to ask, how powerful are social media platforms, and how can they help a writer build a profitable writing career in this digital age?

The Statistics Are Mouth-Watering

Social media has changed the way we live our lives, do our businesses, and market our products and services. Since 2004, social media has grown so fast. Today, it has brought the world to our doorstep. These platforms are now a major source of income, information, and news. In 2020, businesses with online presence grew faster than they had in the previous years. Writers can no longer ignore social media because it's powerful and is here to stay.

Here's the best news; the statistics are mouth-watering. The usage of social media around the world is increasing every day. Humans now spend more time on social media than in previous decades. Users spend an average of three hours per day on social networks. Research by Emarsys 2019, revealed that social media statistics from 2019 show that there are 3.5 billion social media users worldwide. That equates to about 45% of the world population. That number increased to 3.6

billion in 2020 and is projected to increase to 4.41 billion in 2025.

One of the reasons for this high usage of social media is that it is easier for users to access social media using their smartphones. 91% of all social media users access social channels via mobile devices. Wherever you are, you can turn on your data, go to your favourite social media platform, and connect with the world.

Writers Can no Longer Ignore Social Media

As of the year 2020, Facebook is the most widely used social media platform with over 2.32 billion active monthly users. That figure is increasing every day.

90.4% of Millennials, 77.5% of Generation X, and 48.2% of Baby Boomers are active social media users (Emarketer, 2019).

Brands are riding the waves of social media marketing. Businesses now include social media in their marketing strategy and for the right reasons. Social media allows brands to access cost-effective marketing, interact with their audience, and build brand loyalty.

Here's the best part; 54% of social browsers use social media to research products (GlobalWebIndex, 2018). More buyers are joining social media networks and looking for reviews and recommendations. That's why it's essential to have a prominent online presence across various social media platforms.

Social Media Enables You to Build Visibility

The fastest way you can build visibility and create an online presence is through social media. In today's digital world, with the internet and your smartphone, you can easily interact with people all over the world through social media. This is why social media makes people who were not previously known by the public instant celebrities. Today, writers create social media profiles and use several strategies (which I will show you in the next chapter) to talk about their work, connect with readers and promote their books online.

Every day, we see incredible success stories of writers who harnessed the power of social media and used it to create a profitable writing career. I'm a living example. Without social media, I wouldn't have connected with publishers, authors, and readers from different parts of the world. Through Social Media, I built an effective brand as a writer, showed the world my writing skills, and used my strong online presence to promote and sell my works. Without social media, I wouldn't have gotten so many international opportunities as I have. Without social media, I would have remained a shy, newbie writer, struggling to sell his books in the schools in his village.

With social media, I brought the world to my doorstep. I told the world my wishes and dreams, and they listened. You can achieve amazing success in your writing career by harnessing the power of Social Media.

Social Media Enables You to Easily Connect with Readers all Over the World

There are many ways a writer can build a profitable writing career. However, in today's digital world, social media is the fastest and easiest way you can reach your audience and sell your works online. Why? Social media platforms give you lots of options to build your audience, connect directly with your readers, and promote your works with amazing success.

Today, most social media platforms allow you to do a live video broadcast where your audience can see and watch you from wherever they are, and you can speak directly to them as if you are all in the same room. It's a very powerful tool I've used to convert my audience to customers. You can make posts and use them to engage your audience. Through social media, you can join writing communities, connect with writers all over the world, and attract lots of opportunities for yourself. The benefits and possibilities are endless.

Here are the top ten social media platforms for writers
A. Facebook
B. Instagram
C. Twitter
D. Youtube
E. Pinterest
F. Goodreads
G. Linkedin
H. Tumblr

I. Medium

J. Litsy

However, if you are determined to build a profitable writing career using social media, you need to be strategic, or you will not get any results.

In the next chapter, I'll hold you by the hand and show you the ten simple steps you can use to create an effective brand as a writer on social media. When you achieve this, you can harness the power of social media, build the right audience, convert them into customers, and sell your works online.

Writing Exercise

1. What are three things you learnt from reading this chapter that will help you in your writing career?
2. If you decide to build a profitable writing career using social media, which two social media platforms will you focus on?
3. In today's world, writers can no longer ignore social media. Do you agree? If yes, why?

Chapter Three

Building an Effective Brand as a Writer on Social Media

My ringing phone woke me up on Saturday morning. I picked it up. The call was from a client who wanted to publish her book in print with Ifèadigo Publishing Company. We talked for ten minutes, and she promised to make payment during the day. The moment I finished the call, the sunlight that slithered through my window cracks blocked my view. I walked slowly and switched on the two light bulbs in my room.

Next, I walked into the bathroom. I brushed, took my bath, dressed up in my Barcelona Jersey, and went to the gym. When I came back from the gym, I ate breakfast and called my co-founder, Akwaeze Louis, on the phone. We went through our plans for the upcoming week and discussed business strategies. At 1 pm, we did a live broadcast on Instagram where we connected with our clients and readers and told them everything, they'd need to know about Ifèdigo Publishing Company, including our services and future plans. We are building the business and expanding. Our clients are happy at the tremendous progress we had made. The live broadcast was a blast.

The rest of the day moved fast in a blur. When I came back to my house at 5 pm, I was exhausted. Five minutes after walking in through the door, my doorbell rang.

When I opened the door, my eyes widened. "Jasmine," I let out.

Jasmine was my friend. I knew her family. She was a writer. Her family believed she was the next Buchi Emecheta. I knew she was always writing stories. She once told me she had lots of notebooks she hid in her closet. Her family was proud of her. I was proud of her too.

I let her in and went back to my sofa.

Jasmine sat beside me, skipped the pleasantries, and went straight to the point. "I have a problem, Stanley. I believe you are the only one who could help me. Please, I need your help."

My eyes flickered with curiosity. I met her gaze. "What is the problem, Jasmine?"

"Stanley, I have written so many stories. Now I'm ready to come out of my shell and promote my works online. I know everyone thinks I'm shy, but I can do this. I have started since last year, but I'm struggling to build an audience on social media. I want to promote and sell my works online using social media. How do I do this? How do I build an effective brand as a writer on social media? Please, I need your help."

I narrowed my eyes and held her gaze. I was surprised she wanted to do this. I knew Jasmine as a lady who loved to keep to herself. She was shy—yes, but she could talk comfortably when she was with friends and family. Now, she wanted to take her writing to the next level. That was great.

"Jasmine, are you sure you want to do this? I hope no motivational speaker or writing coach is pressuring you to do something you don't want to do."

She shook her head. "I want to be serious about my writing career this year. This is what I need."

I considered her words and said, "Alright, you want to build an audience on social media. Open your Facebook app and give me your phone."

Her eyes widened. It took her a minute to open her Samsung smartphone and her Facebook app. She stared at the device one last time and handed it to me.

My jaw dropped when I stared at her Facebook profile. "It'z Lizzy Baby, who is that?"

"It's me," she replied, as a warm smile appeared on her face.

"That's your Facebook name?"

"Yes."

I read her Facebook bio and frowned. "God's own babe. Small boys, please avoid me. Don't send silly messages on my DM plz."

Oh my God, I thought as I kept scrolling.

I went through her posts, and my jaw dropped. She hadn't posted anything since her last birthday, but her Facebook friends had been dumping their posts on her Facebook timeline.

"Jasmine and 99 others. Jasmine and 30 others. Jasmine and 50 others," I said.

Confusion lined her face. "I don't understand."

I shook my head in sadness. "Of course, you won't. It's so sad that your Facebook profile has become a dustbin."

"How?"

I stared at her. "Instead of asking me how, let me ask you just one question. I assume that your Twitter, Instagram, and other social media accounts are like this. If people go through your Facebook timeline, will they know that you are a writer?"

She looked at me.

I guessed she had begun to understand what it meant to build an effective brand as a writer on social media. For the next thirty minutes, I taught her ten simple ways to build an effective brand as a writer on Facebook. When she left late in the evening, I saw the smile on her face. I didn't need a seer to tell me she would win big in her writing career this year.

The next day, she told me she would like to register and become a member of Stanley's Book Club. I sent the registration details to her, and she registered. Jasmine was ready for 2021.

* * *

Don't be like my friend, Jasmine. Let me share with you ten simple ways to build an effective brand as a writer on social media.

Ten Simple Ways to Build an Effective Brand as a Writer on Social Media

1. Choose the social media platforms that work for you

The moment you decide to come out of your shell and build an effective brand as a writer on social media, choose at least two platforms you are most familiar with, learn how to use them and be active in promoting your brand and connecting with other writers in your niche. For example, I use Facebook, Twitter, and Instagram. I'm very active on

Facebook and Instagram. Choose yours and be active and consistent.

2. *When building an effective brand as a writer on social media, ask yourself three questions:*
   a. Why do I want to write?
   b. What core message am I trying to share on my platform?
   c. How do I want to be perceived?

When you see the name—Stanley Umezulike—on social media, what comes to your mind? Writing, publishing, writing coach, right? This is because I've built an effective brand as a writer on Social Media, and Prolific Fiction Writers Community (PROFWIC), a fast-growing global writing community, is part of that brand.

When you go through my bio and my timeline, you will discover that I'm a publisher, author, and creative writing coach. People connect with me because my content is consistent with my core message and what my brand represents. You should do the same.

Don't create a social media account and begin immediately to tell people to buy your books, products, or services. It won't work that way. Remember, social media platforms are not built primarily for selling. They are designed as a place where people can connect with each other, socialize, and build relationships. Build relationships first. Connect with others. When they like and trust you, they will buy your products.

Here are three types of posts you should make on social media as a writer:
- (a) Posts that connect with your ideal reader (Engagement prompts, conversation starters)
- (b) Posts that captivate your ideal reader (Your short stories, articles that will revolve around your writing niche, for fiction writers—snippets of your fictional world, behind the scenes of the life of a writer)
- (c) Posts that convert your ideal reader into customers (promo posts, sales, invitations)

3. *Clean your Facebook profile*

Do you remember the story of my friend, Jasmine? Her Facebook profile was a dustbin where people dumped their tagged posts. Here's the truth; the Facebook profile of many writers are dustbins. You and 99 others. You and 50 others. Posts like this fill your timeline. Others are shared posts of the religious activities of your pastor, who is also busy promoting his own brand on social media.

Are you the owner of your Facebook timeline, or have you given the people who are tagging you every day on their own posts the control of your Facebook account?

Here's the truth; you are confusing your audience if you keep doing this. How will people know you are a writer if you don't tell them? Here is a question you should ask yourself: if people go through your timeline today, will they know that you are a writer?

If you want to build an effective brand as a writer on social media, clean your timeline. Go to your Facebook setting and change the tagging option so that if someone tags you on their post, you must approve it before it appears on your timeline.

Stop sharing other people's posts except when it is absolutely necessary. Are you helping your pastor to promote his own brand, or are you ready to promote yours? You can't do both.

Your posts should be consistent with who you say you are. If you want to build an effective brand as a writer, your posts should revolve around writing, your core message, and the problems you want to solve for your audience. I've outlined the kind of posts you should make earlier in this piece. Keep your timeline clean and professional.

4. Be authentic

It's sad that many writers use fake names, pictures, and addresses on their social media accounts. They do this and still expect to connect with readers and other writers. Your Facebook name is It'z Periz. You don't have a picture on your profile. In your bio, you stated you live in Houston, in the United States, but one look at your Facebook timeline shows that you live in Sokoto, Nigeria and that everything about you and who you say you are is fake. Worst, you write with chat words and abbreviations instead of writing words in full. If you continue to do this, you can't be able to build a profitable writing career on social media.

Here's my message to you; wake up and be real. In this time and age, your social media profile is your Curriculum Vitae. If it's messed up, you may lose tremendous opportunities because organizations and individuals who would have loved to work with you would decline when they discover you are not authentic.

Use your real name and picture. Your bio should show that you are a writer. Your posts should be consistent with your core message and your brand. Be professional in what you post on social media. Readers want you to be professional. Approach writing with professionalism. With technology and the internet, the world is now at your doorstep. This is the internet. This is social media. You don't know who is watching. Always put your best out there.

5. *Create a content bank*

Building an effective brand on social media requires you to be strategic about creating and publishing content on your chosen platforms. You need to be consistent to build the right audience. You achieve this by creating and posting valuable content in text, audiovisual, and video format. Creating a content bank for posts, you will make in a month or a year will help you save time and effort.

Getting your content organized is key to your social media marketing success. When creating a content bank, create a content calendar. This will enable you to find out the time you will make your posts. It will help you stay productive while on social media instead of scrolling through posts and wasting away time.

Next, create a place to put all your social media content so that you will not lose it. You can use Dropbox or Google drive. All of these will help you create a system that works for you and helps you to make the most out of social media.

6. Infuse storytelling in your content

In today's world, businesses, individuals, and organizations no longer underestimate the importance of storytelling. When you infuse storytelling in your content, it makes it unique, and you will be able to connect more with your audience. Here's the truth, storytelling drives more sales to clients and brands that know how to use it the right way.

Infusing storytelling in your content is different from just posting short stories. Beyond regular content creation, people look for simple stories and personal experiences they can connect with. Brand storytellers know how to use this storytelling element to create content that helps them sell products and services.

7. Attract the right audience

The simplest way to attract the right audience on social media is to make posts that connect with your ideal audience and with writers and readers on Social Media. Remove the wrong people from your friends' list and connect with the right people in your niche. When I started doing this on Facebook, Twitter, and Instagram, I connected with more writers and readers.

Here's the best part, the Facebook and Instagram algorithm started suggesting my profile and my Facebook group to writers and readers and aspiring writers. In less than five months, I discovered I had over 5000 followers, and they were writers, readers, and members of writing communities. For me, this is my ideal audience. But I had to remove many people from my list, except friends and family members, before I could connect with my desired audience.

8. *Join trusted writing communities*

One of the best things about being a writer is being part of a writing community. My journey to building an effective brand as a writer on social media began when I joined writing communities on Facebook. Sometimes writing can be a very solitary affair like a farmer in vast farmland with no other human to help or assist him. When you join writing communities, you will soon find out you are not alone.

The writing community will make you feel like you are a part of a family, a part of a tribe. The best part happens when you begin to connect with experienced writers and begin to learn from them. As a writer, you will discover we are kind souls ready to help and guide each other on the journey.

I advise you to join trusted writing communities online. You can join my writing community on Facebook called Prolific Fiction Writers Community and Writers Helping Writers. You can search for others and join them as well. When you join a writing community, be an active member. Read their rules. Write posts, engage in the posts of other writers. Ask questions, and you will get answers. Learn from those who have passed through your stage in your writing journey. This will definitely transform your writing career.

9. Build long-lasting relationships

Social media will give you the opportunity to come out of your shell and join trusted writing communities like Prolific Fiction Writers Community (PROFWIC) and others. As you do this, connect with writers from all over the world and comment meaningfully on their posts. When people know you support and care about them, they will support and care about you too.

Let me tell you a brief story about my writing career. The people who have given me the greatest support in my writing career are writers and authors from different parts of the world I met online. Here's the shocker, I've not met most of them offline, but we care and support each other as though we've known each other for a long time. That's the power of building meaningful relationships on social media.

Connect with people who have reached where you want to go to, and you will get there faster than you thought. Connect with people who fit your future and disconnect from those who discourage you and no longer fit into your path. Surround yourself with highly productive writers in your niche who have built effective brands as writers on social media and are getting positive results, and continue to learn from them. When you do this, you have the opportunity to be the next writer everyone will celebrate.

10. Create your own Facebook group

As you make progress in building an effective brand as a writer on social media using your Facebook profile for example, there would be a time when you'd discover that you can no longer accept friend requests because you've reached the 5000 friends mark. A Facebook page offers you the opportunity to have many followers, but Facebook has reduced its reach to less than 3 percent. This means you won't reach a wider audience except if you are using paid Facebook advertising. This makes creating a Facebook group a viable option.

Today, there are millions of Facebook groups. However, how you structure your Facebook group will determine whether you will get the results you seek. A word of caution; don't rush to create a Facebook group because others are doing so. Build an effective brand on your personal profile first before creating the right Facebook group. If you don't follow the proper process, you won't get the results you seek.

When you decide to create a Facebook group, here are three questions you should ask yourself:
a) What do I want to achieve by creating this Facebook group?
b) Who is my target audience?
c) Do I have a content creation system that will help me stay consistent in running the Facebook group for a long time?

When you create a highly professional Facebook group, serve your community and help them by providing solutions to their problems. Here's the most important rule: Keep your group content high quality and on target. If it's a Facebook group for writers, teach them, and provide them with resources to help them gain clarity and excel in their writing career. If it's a Facebook group for readers, keep them engaged in book discussions, and offer them information about the world of your characters (for fiction writers) and issues you raised in your book (for non-fiction writers).

When you do this, you will position yourself as an authority in your niche. Your audience would like and trust you and would more than likely buy the books you write. You can easily monetize your Facebook group when you have the right audience and offer them exactly what they need. Remember: help people get what they want, and you will create an opportunity to get what you desire.

Creating my own Facebook group while following this process has helped me build a bigger audience ready to buy and promote my works. You can also use this same strategy to create a YouTube channel, a telegram channel, or other channels on any social media platform of your choice.

When you build an effective brand as a writer on social media, you can get to your destination faster than you thought possible and can achieve amazing success in your writing career. Here's the best news; as you build an effective brand as a writer on social media, you will automatically create the right audience – readers who will keep supporting you and keep buying your books every time you publish your work.

Having an effective brand as a writer on social media can very well translate to having a profitable writing career on social media.

Start today, and do it right—cheers to your success.

Writing Exercise

1. What are the top three things you learnt from reading this chapter?
2. List 5 things you will stop doing right now that are hurting your brand as a writer on social media
3. List 5 things you will do right now that will help you build an effective brand on social media

Chapter Four

Ten Simple Strategies You Can Use to Promote and Sell Your Books on Social Media

Most writers have no idea how to create a buzz and promote their work after writing a great book. Here's the truth; if you don't talk about your book, no one will know you wrote a book.

I get it; most writers would love to just keep writing books and leave the book promotion and marketing to publishers and marketing experts. But here's another truth; you are the best person who can promote and sell your book. When people buy a book or any product, they are not just buying the product; most buy books because they trust the brand which the writer represents. Today, social media has become a marketplace where brands and businesses thrive. Brands and businesses make sales on social media platforms every day.

With the advent of technology, it's now easier to promote and sell your work on social media. Here's the amazing part; you can do it even in the comfort of your room. If you are struggling with promoting your works on social media, these simple and practical strategies can help to get excellent results.

1. Use the preorder strategy

A preorder strategy is a powerful tool you can use to create a buzz around your book and get readers to start preordering before the book's release. Create captivating promotional content, attach your preorder book links to it and share it with your audience on social media.

Most writers struggle to write content for marketing purposes. They just want to write their books and rest. If you are in this category, then you need the services of a copywriter. A professional copywriter will create captivating promotional content that will help sell your book. The promotional content will contain the description or blurb of your book. Once it captures the attention of your readers, they will click the link and preorder your book. On the day of the book release, those who preordered your book will be the first to get it.

2. Use a launch team

One of the most strategic ways to promote your book on social media and get hundreds of people talking about it is by setting up a launch team. A launch team is made up of a group of people that will help you to promote your book and get it in front of a wider audience on social media. They may be your writer friends or members of your audience. Make a post on social media and ask people who are interested to join and be part of your launch team. Their number may be between 1 to 100 or more. The more, the better. You can add them to a Facebook, Whatsapp, or Telegram group. Give them all the details of your book. Their job is to share the promotional content of your book on the day of your book release. They can also start promoting your book to their audience even before the book is published. A launch team will help you get your book in front of a wider audience.

3. *Use online webinar on your chosen social media platforms*

A webinar is an online training. You can organize an online webinar on your chosen platform. It may be on Instagram, Facebook, Telegram, Youtube, Whatsapp, or Youtube, etc., where you have a wide audience. During the webinar, teach your audience one or two important topics from your book and then sell your book to them. The webinar will help them see the value of your book. A well-organized presentation is the tip of the iceberg to entice and hook your audience to read the book.

4. *Use authors and top social media influencers in your niche*

Connect with authors or social media influencers who have bigger platforms than you and request they sell your book to their audience. This is one of the easier ways to get more people to buy your book.

However, to achieve this, you must have built meaningful relationships with them, and therefore they know you. This is why it is important to connect with writers and influencers in your niche. When you connect with each other, it will allow you to collaborate with each other on different projects and support each other in your own businesses.

5. *Share your book reviews written by those who enjoyed your book on social media*

This is one of the best ways to promote your book on social media. Tell readers who buy your book to leave reviews. Then share those reviews across your social media platforms. You can also share pictures of people holding or reading your book. When other readers read and see those who enjoyed reading your book, they will rush to get the same beautiful reading experience.

6. *Get your book reviewed by admins of top Facebook pages that focus on your niche*

Reach out to administrators of top Facebook pages that focus on your niche and request that they read and review your book on your page. This will help boost your book sales.

7. *Attend online speaking events on social media platforms and talk about the issues you discussed in your book*

I encourage writers to learn public speaking, as well. When you write a book, people would see you as an authority on the subject matter you explored in your book. When they invite you to speak at events on their social media platforms, it will be a great opportunity for you to promote your book to their audience by talking about the issues you explored in a way that will capture their interest. When you attend online speaking events, you will reach a wider audience.

8. *Give away a free chapter of your book*

Offer to give away a free chapter of your book. Put the book link at the end of the free chapter. You can host it on a webpage and share the links with your audience on social media. Next, spread the news across all your platforms. Entice your readers to rush to read it. Those who enjoyed it will click to buy to get the whole package.

9. Use paid online advertisement on social media platforms

Facebook, Instagram, Youtube, and other social media platforms now offer brands and businesses the opportunity to pay for online advertisements and use them to promote and sell their products and services to their targeted audience. This is one of the most efficient ways to sell your products on social media and it could generate income.

10. Use affiliate system

Collaborate with top people in your niche who have their own platforms on social media. They get to help you sell your book to their members, and you'd give them a percentage of the profit. Everyone wins. This is why brands and businesses use the affiliate system. It helps you put your book in front of a wider audience.

These simple strategies are highly effective, and they can help you promote your book on social media to sell to millions of readers all over the world.

Writing Exercise

1. What are the three things you learnt about book promotion on social media from reading this chapter?
2. What are three things you will stop doing right now that are hurting your book sales on social media?
3. What are the three things you will start doing now to promote your book on social media?

Chapter Five

Bonus - A Virtual Tour of Stanley's Writing Process

From Idea Generation to Publishing

Writer's note: This is mainly a writing process I use to write my novels. However, non-fiction writers will learn a great deal about book writing by reading this as well.

I have a comprehensive and in-depth writing process. The idea is to make sure I bring out a good story for my readers worldwide.

First of all, before I start working on a story, I'd write the idea down on paper. If there are many story ideas competing for my attention, demanding to be written, I would brainstorm with members of my inner writing circle to avoid falling into the trap of shiny objects syndrome. The productive brainstorming session would help me choose the best story idea from all the ones I have.

Once I've chosen a story idea, I write it down. (I write my stories – first on a notebook and then type on my PC). Next, I create a general outline. Here, I write everything I know about the plot. Usually, as I write this general outline or description of the story, more ideas about the story will enter my mind, and I put them down.

At this point, the story begins to take shape, and I now see the big picture. If some ideas about the story are not clear enough, I put each of them in a question to revisit later. Then I tell someone in my house the story as if it is a movie. Here's what always happens whenever I do this; that person thinks

I'm telling him or her about a film until I say to him or her it's a story I'm working on.

This part is important. When I tell someone the story, if there are gaps or scenes that are not logical, I write them down. Sometimes, I get a better idea at once, and I'd tell the person, "Okay, this other one didn't happen. This is what happened next in the story."

And he or she would usually say, "Yes, this one makes sense."

When I finish telling the person the story, I study the detailed description of the story I've written down, and from there, I create an outline for the prologue or chapter one if the story does not have a prologue.

Next, I write the first chapter of the story. Once I'm through, I get more ideas for the story. That's what usually happens when I start writing. My subconscious mind begins working and supplies ideas that will help me write and finish the story. The real inspiration usually comes when I begin writing, not while I am waiting for it.

After writing the first chapter, I create an outline for chapters two to chapter ten. Next, I write those chapters. Afterwards, I outline chapters ten to twenty and write them. Then chapters twenty to thirty, and write. As I do all of this, I also do the relevant research and get important information and technical details to give my story an air of authenticity.

I follow this process until I finish the story.

At the moment, I write between forty to forty-six chapters, along with a prologue and epilogue. My word count—this started from my last two novels—is usually within the range of 60 - 65,000 words.

A newly completed – unedited – manuscript is called a first draft. When I finish the first draft, I work on the second draft. This means I go back to the beginning of the story, read every word, self-edit, and work on the storyline to ensure there are no missing parts (plot holes).

Here, I would reconstruct the story so that it lives to its full potential. I fix glaring errors, plot holes, wrong sentences, tense mismatch, story structure, scenes that don't make sense, POV, and typos.

If there are areas I couldn't fix immediately, I put them in a red colour in my MS word. When I finish the second draft, I go through it the second time. Here, I reread every sentence and fix all the areas marked in red. I also fix the inconsistencies, plot holes I didn't notice before, make sure the scenes are logical, put important descriptions where they need to be, and make sure the characters' names fit the background and personality of the characters. Otherwise, I change the name of the character.

I would also do this for the setting and other key elements in the story. I flesh out the plot and make sure the story is readable. I also run the story through the Grammarly software and fix the typos (Caution: this software and others similar to it are at best 75% accurate. They by no means replace a professional editor). Once I'm through with this third draft, I send the manuscript to my Alpha reader.

My Alpha reader is an experienced reader who has an eye for detail. He or she will read the story with analytical eyes and provide me detailed feedback, pointing out errors, plot holes, inconsistencies, and things a writer who is too close to their story can't see in their writing.

Then, I go through the story again (fourth draft) and fix the issues he or she observed. I reread every chapter thoroughly.

Next, I send it to Beta readers (usually 4 to 6 Beta readers). Beta readers get a revised manuscript. They would read your manuscript and tell you what worked and what didn't. I usually get beta readers on Beta readers and Critique Groups on Facebook. These groups are made up of writers from different parts of the world. I create a post telling them I need Beta readers for my story. In the post, I indicate the genre and word count to attract those who are interested in my topic. I then send them a DM, chat with them, and email them the first chapter to ensure two things. One, we are a proper fit, and two, they provide the feedback I seek. If the answer to both is a yes, I then send my entire manuscript.

Experienced authors I have within my network also act as my beta readers. Once the beta readers are through with the story, I would study their feedback, go through the story again (fifth draft), and fix the valid issues. I accept only valid observations that are useful for my story. Do keep in mind, you are the author and under no obligation to accept any of the offered suggestions, but don't let your pride override common sense.

When I'm through with the final draft, I read the story one last time and make sure it is in the best shape possible, as my own self-editing skills can allow.

I usually get a title while working on the story. I may change it by the time I'm through with this process. Next, I write the blurb and send the story to my local editor. The blurb is about 150-175 words that tell a bit about the story and has a hook to pull the reader to buy the book. Blurbs are written for the back cover of a paperback book.

Once my editor sends the manuscript back to me, I make the needed corrections and get the manuscript ready for submission (I'll make sure it's properly formatted. I will decide to submit to an agent for traditional publishing or to self-publish using my publishing company).

Next, I write a synopsis and submit both the synopsis and manuscript to my traditional publisher. My publisher requires both. Some publishers require a query letter, the first three chapters of your story, and the synopsis.

If they accept to publish it, and I agree to the contract, I sign the publishing contract and work with the publisher and their in-house editor during the publication process.

At the end of the publication process, the story is published, and a new book is born.

Important Note: Beta readers and editors are very important. Don't skip this process. Don't write and be in a haste to publish. You are too close to your story and can't see all the errors. You need another set of professional eyes to go through your work and help you polish your story and make it shine.

Don't skip this important stage. This is important for writers who want to write for the international audience and get their books in front of the global audience.

Self-editing tips

- ✓ Run an automated grammar and spellchecker – Grammarly, ProwritingAid, Word Rake, etc.
- ✓ Choose simple words.
- ✓ Read your manuscript aloud (or have it read to you).
- ✓ Eliminate unnecessary words: Adverbs, pointless adjectives, and glue words/sticky words such as so, if, than, but, about, in, on, the, was, for, that, of, off, get, just, every, etc. This does NOT mean never use them.
- ✓ Delete redundancies: She thought ~~to herself~~. He clapped ~~his hands~~. She shrugged ~~her shoulders~~. They sat ~~down,~~ or they stood ~~up~~.
- ✓ Eliminate word or phrase over usage and echoes. Also, be aware of your pet words —those you tend to overuse. Use CTRL-F to search for them, then replace as many as possible.
- ✓ Watch out for common word pair mistakes like father/further, affect/effect, less/fewer, etc. Spellcheck, Grammarly, etc., won't catch them.
- ✓ Watch your tenses.
- ✓ Vary sentence structure.
- ✓ Avoid alliteration.
  Avoid quotation marks around words that are not dialogue – commonly used phrases.
- ✓ Avoid passive voice when it's not intentional and deliberate. Look at all sentences with the word "was," and change to active voice: was saying -- change to said. My book was edited by Angie – change to, Angie edited my book.
- ✓ Eliminate clichés.
- ✓ If in doubt, don't capitalize.
- ✓ Subject-Verb Disagreements: If the noun is singular, so must the verb be. Conversely, if the noun is plural, so is

the verb. E.g., The <u>dog</u> **<u>chases</u>** the cat. The <u>dogs</u> **<u>chase</u>** the cat.
- ✓ Homophones: There, they're, their.
- ✓ Make sure your dialogue is properly punctuated, believable, and moves the story forward. Use simple dialogue tags: he said, she said.
- ✓ Avoid name-dropping in dialogue.
- ✓ Maintain a single point of view in each scene. Leave a three-line space between scenes to shift POV.

- ✓ Show don't tell – if what the MC is wearing or the color of the walls is material to the story and moves it forward, then instead of making a list, expose what your MC is wearing and what color the walls are through the MC(s) interaction with their environment.
- ✓ Introduce new characters even with a line or two.
- ✓ Cut anything that doesn't contribute something to the story. I know, we're in love with our words… but maybe we can use this masterpiece line for another story.
- ✓ Delete unnecessary scenes, backstory, background information, etc. They take your reader away from the story.
- ✓ Hand your manuscript to a professional editor after the umpteenth revision and editing. In other words, get it as finished as you can; this frees up the editor to put the final polish on it!

How to pick your editor

Choose a qualified, professional editor. Have the editor go through a sample of your writing and give you feedback. You and the editor must be compatible and can establish a working relationship.

Types of editors:
- ✓ Copy editing - Word-by-word editing that addresses grammar, usage, and consistency issues. Copy editors will check for typos and spelling errors along with correcting grammar, language, syntax errors, and punctuation such as commas, semicolons, and quotation marks.

- ✓ Line editing – Also known as structural editing. It focuses on the finer aspects of language – the flow of ideas, transition elements, tone, and style.

- ✓ Developmental editing – This comes early in the writing process. It addresses setting, timeline, characters, plot, story structure, pacing, and presentation.

- ✓ An editor makes suggestions. You, the author, get to decide whether to accept or not.

- ✓ An editor does NOT change the author's voice. Does NOT change the story.

Writing Exercise

1. What are the three things you learnt about writing after reading this chapter?
2. What are the three things you will stop doing right now that are hurting your writing process?
3. What are the three things you will include in your writing process to help you produce a high-quality book?

Conclusion

Building a profitable writing career on social media takes time, hard work, and consistency, but it's worth the effort. If you are consistent and put in the work, you will achieve amazing results.

To build a profitable writing career, you must invest in your personal growth and writing craft.

Learn every day, read good books, and improve your writing craft. The best strategy will not help a badly written book sell. You can't build a profitable writing career on social media if you are not growing. Growth requires investing your time, energy, and resources.

As you grow and improve your craft, you will build competence and produce top-notch writing your readers will love. This book is my best gift to writers in this digital age.

Thank you for following me on this beautiful journey. I believe the knowledge you've gained from reading this book will help you move with confidence and clarity of purpose in your writing career.

Please, leave a review, where you bought this book. I love to hear from my readers.

I wish you all the best in your writing career.

Cheers to your success.

With love,

Stanley.

About the author

Stanley Umezulike is a Nigerian author, Creative Writing Coach, and Co-founder, IfèAdigo Publishing Company.

He writes family drama, romance, and crime fiction set in tropical Africa. He is a graduate of Political Science from the University of Nigeria, Nsukka, and received his Master's in International Relations at the same University.

In 2016, he wrote and directed a play at Evangel International Secondary School, Kano-Nigeria, while he was a teacher.

In 2019, his novel, Twisted was published by Love Africa Press, a publisher based in Epsom, Surrey, United Kingdom.

His writing has appeared in various publications, including Daily Sun (Nigeria), Creative Freelance Writerz-Africa, Spillwords, and popular online bookstores worldwide.

His new romantic crime fiction novel, Ties That Bind, will be published in 2021 by Love Africa Press.

Stanley is the founder of Prolific Fiction Writers Community, where he helps fiction writers master the art of storytelling. Stanley mentored over 4000 writers within the past two years.

Stanley has been featured in The Light TV Show, Awka, Nigeria, and has been invited to speak on various online and offline platforms.

Through his storytelling, online training, social media posts, messages, books, writings, and fiction writing tutorials in various online and offline platforms, he has transformed lives, helping writers and aspiring writers learn how to write stories for the International audience so they can dominate at the global stage.

Stanley is the cofounder of IfèAdigo, a publishing company that publishes books in print and digital formats, connects authors with global readers, helping them to attain global dominance.

In recognition of his work of transforming lives through storytelling and sharing his stories with the world, Stanley was awarded Top 40 International Leading Youth Award 2020, in the best author of the year Male Category, an initiative organized by Make Mee Elegant Foundation to commemorate the International Youth Day and celebrate youths across the world who have been truly outstanding and impactful in their various fields.

When he is not writing, he enjoys traveling to new places, listening to music, and watching Crime Thriller TV shows. He lives in Nigeria and can be reached via Instagram @stanley_umezulike, Twitter @stanumezulike, Facebook at Stanley Umezulike, and email at umezulike@gmail.com.

Connect with Stanley here:
Join his Writing Community on Facebook:
https://www.facebook.com/groups/profwic/?ref=share
Gmail: umezulike@gmail.com
Whatsapp: ttps://wa.me/message/6BW63HLV7RZDJ1
Twitter: https://mobile.twitter.com/stanumezulike
Instagram:
https://www.instagram.com/stanley_umezulike/

Facebook: https://www.facebook.com/OfficialStanleyUmezulike1/

Okadabooks: https://okadabooks.com/user/stanley_umezulike

Amazon author page: https://www/amazon.com/author/stanleyumezulike

Get his book Twisted from Okadabooks: https://okadabooks.com/book/about/twisted/30199

www.ingramcontent.com/pod-product-compliance
Lightning Source LLC
Chambersburg PA
CBHW030502220526
45464CB00006B/2616